START

POORLY

Sidestepping Perfection to Reach Your Goals

Justin Grifford

"The overarching point of *Start Poorly* is simply 'To Start!' We all need to set aside our inhibitions and take that leap of faith that could change us forever. This book outlines a clear and simple approach that will carry the reader from start to finish as they chase their dreams."

Rick Dinkins
Brigadier General, USAF (Retired)

"Justin puts a new spin on an age-old problem that almost all of us are faced with when tackling a life challenge or chasing a dream or goal. What's even more refreshing is that there is no fluff; he gets right to matter at hand with a simple but clear blueprint for success!"

Mark Smith
President & CEO of CPI Group

"Justin lays out a plan for you to get your butt off the couch and get moving. In *Start Poorly*, you'll be given permission to fail, permission to pause and permission to suck. But you'll be inspired to keep moving and you'll be armed with steps to get where you desire to go... the world around you needs you in tip top shape – conquering battles that are meaningful to you. Go get it!"

Clint O'Neal
Executive Director, Arkansas Economic Development Co.

"Life is full of things we struggle with, yet we must push through and improve. That is what *Start Poorly* emphasizes. I love how you compare goal setting to a marathon. I was encouraged reading this because it reminded me that even though beginnings may be rough, they can still lead to success. What I took from this book was to not get discouraged of failure but embrace it because this is part of the process of growth.

Josh Austin
Head Coach of Men's Basketball, Williams Baptist University

Start Poorly: Sidestepping Perfection to Reach Your Goals

Copyright © 2024 by Justin Grifford

ISBN   Paperback   979-8-9915738-0-1

         E-Book   979-8-9915738-2-5

         Audiobook   979-8-9915738-1-8

I dedicate this book to my wife, Stacie, who has seen me start poorly more times than we are both willing to admit. Your encouragement and feedback throughout this process are without match. I love you.

Table of Contents

Introduction

W hen was the last time you were horrible at something? I'm talking embarrassingly bad. Unsure? Ask your parents, your spouse, or your closest friends. Was it the first time you picked up a racquet? Tried a new card game? Cooked a new dish?

Life is full of things we're not good at. From parallel parking to flossing regularly to eating healthier, we all have things we struggle with. When possible, we tend to avoid them. Parents often wish they were more consistent in disciplining their children. You might wish you could get to bed earlier so you can wake up on time or be more frugal and not spend so much. The list of things we fall short on is long, filled with things that don't matter to those that do.

Yet, life is full of things we must do. We must go to school. We must go to work. We have to parent. Not doing those things creates another slew of problems we want to avoid, so we do them.

But if the classroom isn't your thing, tough luck—the work still has to get done. If you're not great at budgeting or paying bills, too bad; it still needs to be handled, your 20 subscription services won't cancel themselves after all.

The reality is this: everything you've ever started; you were terrible at. Whether you were a chess prodigy or had a natural golf swing, you began knowing nothing. From learning to ride a bike to tackling algebra, from potty training to tying your shoes—life is full of things we initially don't do well. So, if the things we're bad at are optional, we choose not to do them. But in life, some things aren't optional, and we have to push forward, done poorly or not.

Can you relate? Think of some of your own poor starts. Chances are, the first time you ever did something, it wasn't great. It was probably terrible. Maybe it was okay. Likely, it was poor. The point is we all have poor starts. I'll share one of mine.

I've grown into the type of person who really likes goals and sets weekly and yearly goals for myself. Most goal-setters love the end of one year and the start of the next. To all the dreamers out there, January 1st is the starting point to launch into something you have always wanted to do or to double down on what you are already doing.

- If it's running, more miles!
- If it's reading, more books!
- If it's dental hygiene, more flossing!

I recently started the new year off poorly.

If I could personify my goals, I would describe them as a marathon runner about to move at the sound of the starting pistol. If this is the case, my

January 1st was a stray dog that peed down my ankle into my running shoes, only then to trip me at the starting line.

Nothing went right.

On January 1st, I was one of the many unlucky winners of the COVID/Flu combo, leaving me dizzy, fatigued, and battling pounding headaches. The books I planned to read sat untouched, collecting dust, because it's hard to focus on words that spin. As for my workouts? They were laughable—just walking to the bathroom and back felt like a full-body exercise.

Sure, most people have gone through something similar and eventually recovered. What didn't help, though, was a pulled hamstring followed by an infection that left me hobbling around for the rest of the year. These problems are minor compared to what many face on a daily basis, but the point is that I had intended the start of my year to look much different. It wasn't the start I was hoping for. I started poorly. But a poor start is still a start.

Why should you read this?

This is a book about chasing dreams, completing goals, developing habits, and being terrible at them. At first, anyway. This book will encourage you to stumble and trip over your own feet as you move toward the goals you've always wanted to achieve. It won't always be graceful. In fact, it will often feel discouraging, as if you're making no progress at all. But even a stumble has direction, and it might as well be taking you toward the things you've always dreamed of doing.

It's time to do something about the dreams you have. This book will give insight, research, and practical steps to overcome mental, practical, and psychological roadblocks that stand in your way. It will help you sidestep perfectionism and overcome fear that paralyzes your progress. But how is this book different from others in its genre? My hope is that the contents of this book will be mildly familiar but refreshingly different.[1]

My promise to you is that this book is not bloated with repetition. Some of the best books out there on setting goals and creating new habits have solid gold tips but give countless ways to implement them. Helpful but not always necessary. I will do my best to use five words, whereas others might use ten. You can love it or hate it, but you should be able to finish it rather quickly. If anything, I believe brevity can create greater retention.

Let's stumble into Chapter 1.

Part 1: The Problem

8

1

Always Late

People are doing what you have always wanted to do. Let that sink in for a moment.

It's easy to look up and notice the excellence around you and the progress others are making in life. Maybe not around you per se, because the people you rub shoulders with aren't exactly the pinnacle of human achievement. But there are people who have our attention: artists, musicians, writers, entrepreneurs, and athletes. People with charm and charisma, each of them living out the goals and dreams they have set out to accomplish.

Most of them now have the means to pursue whatever they want whenever they want. Maybe those were dreams we had as kids, but life looks different now. But even today, we wake up feeling like we are late for something ·that life has passed us by.

You're okay with not being Patrick Mahomes and winning multiple Super Bowls. You're content with not being Elon Musk and worth billions. You're fine if you're not a bestselling author like J.K. Rowling, and you're satisfied if you don't tackle life with the same intensity as David Goggins... But you might have expected to be a bit further along by now, didn't you?

Late again!

A friend gets married and starts a family sooner than you. A colleague in your field was making what you are NOW making ten years ago, and you are just starting to catch up. She made partner when you wanted to. He is training for that marathon you have always wanted to run. You don't have the money saved up for retirement that financial experts say you should have. Your neighbors' kids have been working on scholarship applications for months, and yours haven't started. Life presents many instances that give us the feeling that we are always running behind. Not late to a meeting or late for work but **late to life's milestones.**

While I don't believe jealousy and envy should be long-term motivators in life, they can reveal a level of discontent. These feelings expose a sense of angst and yearning—not necessarily for what others have or are doing, as this book isn't about comparing yourself to others or keeping up with the Joneses. However, seeing others succeed and achieve their goals can remind you of your own aspirations. Even if your goals and dreams are different, you still want to achieve them.

That angst is about YOU finally doing what YOU have always wanted to do. There's a yearning inside for more. A desire to do something you've never done. With the angst is frustration and perhaps a long litany of failed attempts that taunt you. This angst is the tension between where you are and where you desire to be. Who you are and who you desire to become.

You don't have to be late anymore. You don't have to wonder what it's like. You have a responsibility to do something about it.

Potential by the numbers

Author Jon Acuff, in his book *All it Takes is a Goal,* surveyed 3000 people and found that 50% believed that ONLY half of their potential has been tapped. Acuff compared this to waking up on Christmas morning only to open half of your presents and leaving the rest under the tree.[1]

These figures leave a lot of potential on the table. But if this describes you, you are not alone. There is something we miss when we don't live up to our full potential. It's costing us. When we leave life and potential up to chance, we have no way of steering ourselves to the left or to the right. We give up control, and life just happens to us rather than us taking action. The way we live further into our potential is to dream a little and set goals of where we want to go and who we want to be.

What is the sum cost of a life without dreams and goals? It might be costing you more than you think. Have you ever stopped to consider that not pursuing a dream or fulfilling a goal might be affecting your health? Costing you money, fulfillment, order, direction, self-respect, or peace? And at the end of the day, from the person living in third-world slums to the billionaire living in Malibu, we all want peace, comfort, and joy in our lives.

Back to the Research

Of those 3000 surveyed, 70% of those asked about their potential said they had had **moments** where they felt they were living up to their potential.

In other words, for just a **moment** here and there throughout their life, they tasted it. They felt it. They had that surge of energy run through them. They discovered what it's like to savor it and starve for it again.

If you are part of that 70%, you have loved those moments. In those moments, you felt like an equal at the table of greats. You have felt, even for a moment, like you belong. At that moment, the world is not passing you by, and you are no longer late. When you believed for so long that only the best belonged at that table, you discovered what it was like to sit there.

Pull up a chair, you have a seat at the table.

3 Questions to Start Poorly

- What are three areas of life in which you feel late or behind?
- Have you had a moment where you were living up to your potential? What were you doing, and what was that like?
- Who are some of the people that sit at the table you want to sit at? What will it take you to join them?

2

What Stops You

W e can easily see the problem created when we stop short and choose not to live in all that we are capable of doing. So, what stops you? What stops any of us?

Fear.

The answer is easy. You can argue time, but the truth is you are fearful that it will be a waste of time. If you disagree with this, keep reading. You could say money, but only because you are fearful it will waste money. In this case, all roads lead to fear. Fear comes in many forms, and it will feed you a bunch of junk and garbage.

Fear Court

Do you remember when indoor malls were a thing? I'm talking about the indoor malls where you could see Santa, run through American Eagle, and snag a soft pretzel, all within 200 feet of one another. With indoor malls came food courts, a taste bud wonderland. You could order a slice of Sbarro Pizza while your friend got Lo Mein and an egg roll. The mall food court had so many options. Fear serves you in a similar way. In the food court of fear, there are plenty of vendors for you to spend your physical, mental, and emotional funds. If you feed fear, fear will feed you. Unfortunately, we frequently indulge in the buffet of "what ifs" and "worries," on a daily basis. Like a food court, fear offers many options and has multiple personalities. It can shift its nature at any moment, and if you allow it to dictate your actions, you will find yourself being pulled in many directions.

Fear says many things. When considering your dreams and goals, fear tells you to sit down and shut up and leave the job for important people, the smart people, the talented people, those with natural ability...the people who are not you.

If you took a step toward your goal, fear will then tell you, "You have no idea what you are doing!" It will tell you everyone is in a league far beyond where you are. Even when you overcome one kind of fear and choose to pursue your goal, fear will then tell you as you get somewhat decent at it that you have to know everything about it and question you on why you are not better yet. Fear accuses, "Why have you not mastered this yet? There are so many people out there better than you at this."

Fear tells you lies, steals your confidence, and accuses you of not being dedicated. Whether it be the fear of what others might think and say or the fear of not doing it perfectly, fear is a powerful force.

Fear Paralyzes

If you have ever seen an old depiction of a lion tamer at the circus, you've likely seen the lion tamer holding a whip and a stool. (I once read Christopher Walken was a lion tamer in a circus act. Have fun with that.) While we might think the whip is the most important tool to have with a lion, it is instead the stool. When the lion tamer lifts the stool and points the legs toward the lion it freezes. When a lion looks at the multiple legs, it is unable to focus on one at a time and is instead paralyzed with the inability to focus on just one.

Fear has a similar effect. We can get bogged down so much with "what if" that it paralyzes us from taking action. We look for reasons "not to" based on any given fear.

Ruts and Highways

Thoughts create pathways in your brain. The frequency and intensity with which we think of these thoughts create a longer, wider pathway. A single thought is the equivalent of a small rabbit trail, almost naked to the human eye if walking through woods. Thinking the same thought often turns that same rabbit trail into a running trail, wider and longer. More time spent pondering can transform that running trail into a gravel road, then a paved road, then a 2-lane road, until it becomes a 4-lane highway. Fear is no different. But instead of highways, fear creates ruts.

When I was a kid, my family hunted land in South Arkansas, and there was a 4-wheeler trail that took us to the camp house. The roads flooded often, and there were ruts well established for years that you knew you had to drive to get through. Even when you tried to drive over them, your wheels fell into place, and you had to stay in the ruts. "You belong in the ruts," the roads would say.

Fear will try to tell you the same. You may have a dream, a goal that your thoughts have built a mental highway towards, but fear continually will say, "No, get in these ruts because that's where you belong. Let the other drivers go by. This is not for you."

Facing Fear

Every religion, life philosophy, area of study, or discipline is in agreement on fear. Fear must be confronted.

Christians take their cues and commands from the Bible, which encourages us to 'fear not' in various forms up to 365 times—one for each day of the year. Stoic philosophers like Marcus Aurelius and Seneca the Younger wrote, "Never let the future disturb you," and "We suffer more in our imagination than in reality."

Cus D'Amato, renowned boxing coach of Mike Tyson, once said of fear, "Fear is like a fire. You can make it work for you. It can warm you in winter, cook your food when hungry, give you light when you are in the dark, and produce energy. Let it go out of control, and it can hurt you, even kill you. Fear is a friend of exceptional people."

William Shakespeare once said, "Of all the base passions, fear is the most accursed." The twice recipient of the Nobel Peace Prize for her discoveries in radioactivity, Marie Curie once quipped, "Nothing in life is to be feared; it is only to be understood. Now is the time to understand more so that we may fear less." I even wore a "No Fear" t-shirt in middle school to let people know I meant business.

From religion to stoic philosophy into the world of sports, literature, middle school, and science, all areas of life agree... Fear must be confronted and understood if we are to move forward in life.

The more real the threat, the more heroic your actions. So how do you confront fear? How do you cut fear off at its knees?

Take one single step. *Start poorly.*

3 Questions to Start Poorly

- What vendor often feeds you from the Fear Court?
- In which areas of life does fear paralyze you?
- What ruts does fear tell you that you belong in?

Part 2: The Solution

Start Poorly

If you feel late, what can catch you up? If you feel behind, what will push you ahead? If fear always stops you and pulls you into ruts, what will restart you and push you out?

I propose two words that conveniently title this book:

Start Poorly

Sidestep perfection and give yourself permission to be terrible at something.

By starting, you take action. By starting, you are doing something about the gap that exists between where you are and where you want to be. By starting, you put yourself in the driver's seat. You become the master of your own destiny. By starting, you begin dictating the terms and taking control. By **starting poorly**, you do not have to be a pro; you don't even have to be all that good at it. By starting poorly, you cut fear off at its knees.

Fear vs. Start Poorly

Since fear often presents us with many conflicting headlines, we should consider starting poorly as a strategic advantage. This approach allows us to harness the potential of embracing imperfection.

Fear says, "You lack the skill and talent to do this." Starting Poorly says, "I know, I'm just getting started." Fear then shifts gears and says, "Well, if you are going to do this, you need to pick this up quickly." Starting Poorly says, "I don't have to be any good at this. I just started and I can go at any pace I like."

Fear says, "Even IF you start, you'll never be as good as them." Starting Poorly says, "I'm not them. They've been doing this for a long time." We often make the mistake of comparing our beginnings to someone else's long-established success. Never compare your beginning to someone else's middle.[1] Fear wants you to freeze with hesitation. Starting Poorly says, "There is no need to hesitate; I'm just taking a small step."

Fear says, "If you start, you have to be perfect, and you cannot miss a day. If you miss a day working on your goal, then you aren't really dedicated." Starting Poorly says, "If I miss a day, I can pick it back up tomorrow." Starting Poorly allows you to sidestep perfection to chase your dreams, complete your goals, and develop your habits. Perfection can wait.

Fear attacks from multiple sides in multiple ways, ready to serve you the meal of the day. Starting Poorly declaws fear by taking simple steps- 1 minute at a time at the pace that you decide. Fear also wants to weigh in on your commitment level. Fear says, "If you are not sold out to working on your goal at LEAST 5 hours a day, you are not committed!"

Nope.

A poor start means I can start by only dedicating 15 minutes a day if I want to. Maybe just 5 minutes. It's a poor start, after all, but it's still a start. The Fear Court is ready to serve you with multiple options to choose from. But Start Poorly packs its own lunch.

Fail Big

Two-time Oscar winner Denzel Washington, in his widely shared commencement address at Dillard University, advised the graduates to "Fail Big." [2]

"Fail big, you only live once, do what you are passionate about.... Don't just aspire to make a living; aspire to make a difference."

He concludes by telling the graduates to "Fall Forward." Dreams that have no path planned toward them are just dreams and will only fuel disappointment.

In another address, Washington notes how baseball Hall of Famer Reggie Jackson struck out 2600 times in his career, the most in the history of baseball. But we don't remember him for strikeouts; we remember his homeruns. Thomas Edison conducted over 2,000 failed experiments before making the lightbulb work.[3] Yet, we do not remember his multiple failures but this one great success. Each failure was a fall forward.

Starting poorly is not just a fall forward but also a fail forward. It's about learning from trying, failing, and picking yourself up to try again. It's the first small, imperfect step toward the goal or dream you've always had.

Leverage Failure

Entrepreneur and founder of Spanx Sara Blakely, on failure: "When my brother and I were growing up, my father would encourage us to fail. We'd sit around the dinner table, and he'd ask, "What did you guys fail at this week?" If we had nothing to tell him, he'd be disappointed. The logic seems counterintuitive, but it worked beautifully." [3]

She goes on to say, "He knew that many people become paralyzed by the fear of failure. They're constantly afraid of what others will think if they don't do a great job and, as a result, take no risks. My father wanted us to try everything and feel free to push the envelope. His attitude taught me to define failure not as failing to achieve the right outcome but as not trying something I want to do."

You only fail when you refuse to start poorly.

Hit the Spinner

With three kids in the house, we have a closet full of board games. One of the games in the rotation is Chutes and Ladders. Chutes and Ladders is a game with 100 ascending squares and a spinner ranging from 1·6. Throughout the board are ladders that allow you to climb higher, bypassing multiple squares and chutes that drop you down sometimes 10 to 20 squares. The first player to reach the top wins.

Mathematically, it is possible to never finish a game and be stuck in the "chute and ladder" loop forever. But, of all the games I have played, I have always finished. Every time I played, I reached the end. The only occasion I didn't was when a kid got upset and threw a fit and quit. It happens.

Life is a lot like a game of Chutes and Ladders, and so are your goals. While it may seem like you could be stuck in an endless loop of moving forward only to have major setbacks, **as long as you don't quit, you will reach the top.**

You will have days working toward your goal, like ladders where time flies by, and your progress is energizing and fruitful. You'll run the mile faster, break a creative block, get lots of views on a video you made, or bring on multiple new clients. While other days will be like chutes, and you feel a regression. The mile is slower. You have a cheat day and feel awful the next day. You stare at the flashing prompt on your Word document and have nothing to write. We've all been there.

Start Poorly. Hit the spinner. When you hit the spinner, you will always move forward. Don't give up. You will get there. Even if you land on one every time, you will reach the top.

Laughably Simple

In their book *Streaking*, Jeff and Jami Downs highlight that one key factor in maintaining a habit streak is to make the goal or action laughably simple. Their advice is to start with embarrassingly small goals and gradually increase them over time, if necessary.[4] Cayla Croft from Mommy Millionaires calls these messy immediate actions. Small steps help you improve gradually and move a bit further. For instance, practicing the piano for just five extra minutes each day adds up to 30 hours of extra practice by the end of the year. Similarly, saving $5 a week amounts to $260 by year's end. Keep it simple and keep it small.

Laughably simple, embarrassingly small goals, and messy immediate actions all drink from the same fountain as Start Poorly. Your actions and steps don't have to be pretty; they don't have to be precise. That can all wait till much later. Progress beats perfection every time. For now, face the direction you want to go, stumble, fail forward, and start poorly.

3 Questions to Start Poorly

- What is something you want to start?
- Can you think of an area of your life or work where you had to continually hit the spinner until you made progress on something?
- What big gains (ladders) or major setbacks (chutes) did you encounter?

4

The Science of Confidence

I often find that the science presented in habit-forming and goal-setting books can be a bit overdone—interesting, but not always practical. So, I'll take a chance and share my own perspective based on what I've found helpful. I believe this concept can strengthen your resolve.

Meet Self-Efficacy.

Self-Efficacy (SE) is defined as an individual's belief in their capacity to act in certain ways necessary to reach specific goals. SE is about confidence and belief in yourself.

A person with a high SE sees challenges as things to be mastered and conquered rather than things to be avoided. They recover from failure faster. If they score low on tests, they determine they did not prepare well enough. They feel they possess more agency when it comes to goals and challenges.

A person with a low SE views challenges as personal attacks to be avoided. When a task is too difficult, they focus on the skills they lack rather than the ones they possess. If they score low on tests, they determine the test was simply too difficult.

If you have to choose between the two, it's an easy decision: we all want high SE. The good news is that you aren't stuck with a fixed SE score; you have the power to raise it or lower it (though, ideally, you'll want to raise it). How is this possible?

To put it simply, to enhance your self-efficacy, you should aim for an 80% success rate. But what does that mean?

The 80% Rule

In a study done with students in a classroom, it was found when a student was able to grasp and retain 80% of the material, he/she would have the ability and confidence to learn the remaining 20%.[1]

80% became a benchmark. 80% retention created an internal confidence to take ownership and learn the remaining material. The teachers could trust the students to learn the remaining 20% of material. This principle is also used when leaders look to delegate tasks and responsibilities. Leaders are told: Find someone who can do it about 80% as good as you and then hand off that task if you desire. The person chosen can be trusted to grow into that task.

This is also true of goal setting. One way to tell if your goal is too difficult or too easy is the 80% rule. Are you completing 100% of your goal week in, week out? If you are, great! But is it too easy? Do you feel challenged at all? If not, it's likely your goal is too easy.

Are you only completing 50-60% of your goal? If so, it's likely your goal is too difficult. A goal that is too easy is not a challenge; a goal that is too difficult is defeating and deflates confidence. If you want to build your SE, aim for the 80% mark and use that benchmark to manage your goals from week to week.

For example:

- If your goal is to read 100 pages in a week and you typically manage only 50 to 60, then your goal may be too high. Consider lowering it to 75 pages. Now, if you read 60 pages, that's 80% of your revised goal, which means you only need to read 15 more pages to reach 100%.

· If you want to run 10 miles each week and routinely run 9 to 10 and want to challenge yourself more, raise it to 12 or 13 miles.

· If your goal is to practice guitar every day for 30 days in a month, but you only manage to practice for 15 days, this can be discouraging over time and may hinder your progress and confidence. Instead, adjust your goal to 20 days.

Rome wasn't built in a day. A little science in your corner can set you up and build confidence for the long haul. Small, incremental steps to build confidence are exactly what my friend Jimmy did in the next chapter.

3 Questions to Start Poorly

- When something doesn't go your way, do you often blame yourself or your circumstances?
- Would you say you have a low SE or a high SE?
- How can you use the 80% rule to raise your SE?

5

Couch to Kilimanjaro

I n 2018, Jimmy found himself overweight, weak, and devoid of passion. He described himself as both apathetic and pathetic, humorously remarking that he wasn't out of shape—"round is a shape." A shadow of the athlete he once was, Jimmy had an impressive resume but felt uncertain about his future. He had traveled the world and met hundreds of interesting people, each with their own passions, yet he lacked a clear path forward for himself—no vision of what lay ahead. His health was declining, and so were his passions, dreams, and goals.

However, deep inside him was this tiny ember of a dream burning 20 years in the making. He wanted to climb the highest point in Africa. So, he decided to start poorly.

He told his wife Beth that he planned to go from the couch to Kilimanjaro in 1 year. He knew he had to take steps. He reasoned, "I can't climb Kili until I can run a marathon. And I can't run a marathon until I can run a half-marathon."

So, he signed up for a half-marathon in April 2019, giving himself six months to prepare. In the worst-case scenario, he would revert to his old self, lose the money he spent on the race, and still hold the title of King of His Couch.

With six months to train, he hit the pavement on day one for his first run. He recalls that he could only manage to run a quarter of a mile before needing to stop. So, he walked. But walking wasn't quitting.

He didn't quit. Instead, he set embarrassingly small goals, knowing that pushing too hard could lead to injuries that would sideline him for days or even weeks. Jimmy made sure to challenge himself just enough each day to continue training. He completed the half marathon, then the full marathon, and on January 21st, 2020—one year and 11 days after his first run (which he might call a stumble)—he stood at the summit of Kilimanjaro.

Jimmy posted on Facebook about that moment: "I've spent a lot of time reflecting on that first run. I was scared, frustrated, and embarrassed, but somehow, I did it anyway."

As of the writing of *Start Poorly*, Jimmy has traveled to the summit of Kilimanjaro 3 times and recently completed a marathon at the base of Mt. Everest, the world's highest marathon.

Dreams Unlocked

Kilimanjaro was a dream... Mission accomplished!

What came next was unexpected. Fulfilling the Kili goal made him feel alive, and he thought to himself that people would pay money to have this experience. To overcome fears, complete these kinds of goals. To reach deep inside and take on a challenge that demanded everything from them.

Fulfilling the Kili dream unlocked an idea for him. It unlocked Discipletrek. Discipletrek is an organization that offers faith-based adventure tours to some of the most spectacular locations on the planet. At the writing of this book, Discipletrek has over a dozen trips planned for the future. Although it's not quite a full-time job yet—Jimmy believes it will be by 2025—he feels energized and alive doing something he loves alongside others, helping them fulfill and overcome their own dreams and challenges. For more information on Discipletrek, visit discipletrek.org.

Kilimanjaro, Discipletrek began with a little desire and a poor start. Running a quarter of a mile and walking the rest. While on one excursion, he made the following comments on Facebook:

"You're finished. C+ work will change more lives than your A+ work, which never gets done. So many people are waiting till they can do something perfectly to take action, but you need to just start. **Start poorly**...*after time, you'll get better, and if you keep waiting, you'll never ever get where you want to be.."*

Jimmy agrees. Start Poorly.

This didn't happen for him overnight. But it started with a little grit and an alarm clock. From humbled to hopeful.

<u>Humble Beginnings</u>

Some of the most successful actors, entrepreneurs, writers, and musicians have what they would call very humble, if not poor starts. There is something we love about humble beginnings. We love to watch what they have overcome and how they remained grounded as they rose to prominence. It's inspiring to witness the role that humble beginnings had in shaping who they are today.

This is why we love the story of Rocky—a struggling, unknown fighter with grit and perseverance. Each Rocky movie features a training sequence that shows his initial clumsy movements, followed by a montage of him becoming faster, stronger, and tougher. He outruns Apollo, chases a chicken, and runs up the iconic steps of the Philadelphia Museum of Art. We witness his humble beginnings and his rise to the top.

In J.R.R. Tolkien's *The Lord of the Rings*, Aragorn is written as a humble and lowly Ranger from the north. It is through the relationships and reputation he builds among races of Middle Earth as wise, kind, and brave that he takes his rightful place in the bloodline of rulers as the King of Gondor. Whether fictional or real, we love these stories.

It's why we love the story of King David, who was overlooked as the next king of Israel. When all his brothers lined up for the prophet Samuel's visit, David's father left him in the field to tend sheep, believing his son would not be chosen. David rises from shepherd to warrior to king. A poor and humble start indeed.

It's why we love the story of Harry Potter author J.K. Rowling. In her 2008 commencement speech to Harvard graduates, she described a point in her life where she had failed on an epic scale. Her exceptionally short marriage fell apart. She was an unemployed single mother and considered incredibly poor for the standards in England. Rowling said,

"I began to direct all my energy into finishing the only work that mattered to me. Had I really succeeded at anything else, I might never have found the determination to succeed in the one arena I believed I truly belonged. I was set free because my

greatest fear had been realized, and I was still alive, and I still had a daughter whom I adored, and I had an old typewriter and a big idea. And so rock bottom became the solid foundation on which I rebuilt my life." [1]

There is a long list of people we know from the moments they hit big, not from their poor starts:

· Country Musician Luke Combs didn't learn to play guitar until he was 21.

· KFC's Colonel Sanders was in his 60s when he began driving across the country selling his chicken recipe to gas stations.

· Samuel L. Jackson didn't star in Pulp Fiction until he was 45. Alan Rickman didn't fall from Nakatomi Plaza until he was 42. If you know... you know.

· Even Rev. Billy Graham is said to have preached his very first sermon for only 8 minutes (many patrons of long-winded preachers might consider this a great and welcomed start versus a poor one).

Our world is full of successful people with humble beginnings who started poorly even later in life. Whether you start from a deficit, from less-than-ideal health with little to no money, or start from a later stage in life, it's never too late.

Forced to Start Poorly

Consider again all the other areas of life where you have no choice but to start poorly. In a new job, you won't be as effective on day 1 as you will be on day 100. Even if it's in your field, you must navigate new dynamics and relationships. If you have children, your parenting skills develop over time, especially during those first few sleepless nights when the baby wants to play at 2 a.m. Learning how to properly budget takes time.

If you want to start running, you might look an awful lot like Jimmy and start poorly. If you want to lift weights, you are going to need to start light. If you want to buy or sell a house for the first time, you have no idea what you are doing. Talk to someone who has experience or get a realtor to help you. If you want to learn how to edit and upload videos, I bet your first one is going to be awful, with poor sound and lighting.

That's okay.

You are already forced to start poorly in so many areas of life, so why not start poorly on something you have always wanted to do? What if you set out like Jimmy did? What if you took a dream, dormant for years, and turned it into an action?

In the next section, I have laid out 5 phases in which I believe every dream, goal, or habit resides.

3 Questions to Start Poorly

- Whose humble beginnings do you admire?
- What things do you recall as a child doing for the first time and being horrible at?
- What is a long-term goal or dream you have always had tucked away in your mind for "someday"?

58

Part 3: The Phases

Intro to the Phases

5 Phases to Start Poorly

E very dream you wish to fulfill, every goal you want to achieve, and every habit you aim to form will take you through five different phases. These are stages you might enter and struggle to move beyond—points on a map that you may visit but never truly leave.

1. Dream Phase
2. Plan Phase
3. Start Phase
4. Grind Phase
5. Finish Phase

While I don't think identifying these phases is revolutionary, I do believe they give you a gauge as to where you are. Maybe you are a lot further along in the process than you think you are. Or maybe you find yourself stuck in one phase far longer than you thought.

In the next chapters, I will outline what I identify as five distinct phases of dream chasing and goal pursuit. Each chapter will include an overview of the phase along with its defining characteristics. We'll examine the pros and cons of each phase, as well as the feelings and fears you can expect to encounter. The Fear Court from Chapter 2 will be fully operational during these five phases, ready to serve you the 'fear of the day' special. I'll provide tips on how to thrive in each phase to help set you up for success.

I'll also introduce what I call 'box jumps.' When I played football in high school (or, more accurately, when I was on the team), we had to do box jumps to improve our explosiveness and leg strength. I hated box jumps and tried to avoid them, but I couldn't progress until I completed them. Box jumps would delay my workout and prevent me from moving forward.

For the purpose of analogy, box jumps are what keep you from moving from one phase to the next. I'll identify box jumps that exist between phases and show you how to clear them.

Let's start with the Dream Phase.

6

The Dream Phase

Most people picking up this book and cracking open the pages are doing so because they are in the Dream Phase, and they don't know what to do about it.

To be fair, maybe using the word dream romanticizes it a little. But whether it's a dream, a goal, or a habit you want to develop, I believe they all follow a similar formula.

THIS THING is the dream, the habit, the goal. When you're at work, you think about it. When you lie awake at night, you think about what it would be like. Not all the time, but often enough. It excites you. You imagine a life where this is now complete. A life where you are living in this alternate image of yourself. You ponder how you will feel when you achieve it. It's the What IF.

What if you:

- ran the marathon
- started the business
- created the YouTube channel
- wrote the book
- learned the instrument
- lost the weight
- earned the degree
- planted to garden
- started the support group
- earned your builder's license

Pros of the Dream Phase

The Dream Phase is fun because you can do anything and be anyone. One of the great fun things about the Dream Phase is that you can think as big as you like. Imagine being a huge success at whatever you do. You can think outside the box, and it's exciting because the sky's the limit. It's a wonderland of positivity and possibility. It's those fleeting but confident thoughts where you slowly scratch your chin and look up to the left and say to yourself, "Yeah, I could do that."

When you believe you can do hard things, even for just a moment, you get a taste of a dream you might have. It's like being a kid and wanting to be an astronaut or a professional baseball player all over again.

You start to tell yourself that you could do it too. You could be successful as well, and you could do it your way. Imagine how YOU would treat your employees if YOU started a business, how YOU would promote your channel, or what races YOU could enter. In other words, YOU envision how YOU would put your unique stamp on it. I realize I've probably overused the all-caps YOU at this point.

This is the fun phase where you can be anything and do anything, and it costs you nothing—not a cent. There's no hard work involved. No getting up early. In your mind, everything goes perfectly! It's just a happy little world and persona you've created for yourself. But therein lies the problem: it exists only in your head.

Cons of the Dream Phase

The biggest drawback of the Dream Phase is that you can stay in Wonderland forever—sometimes for years or even a lifetime. Millions of people around the world never take a single step toward their dreams or big goals. Over time, Wonderland can turn into a prison they're afraid to escape. The dream can feel so vast that you may convince yourself it's meant for someone else, not for you.

Like in every phase, we will discuss how fear plays a role in keeping you from going anywhere. At each phase, fear manifests itself in a different way.

Tips to Thrive in the Dream Phase

#1. Do what YOU want

Pursue your goal, pursue your dream, and not someone else's dream. Set goals that are truly your own and not what someone else wants you to do. You'd be surprised by how many things people do simply because others want them to, not because they genuinely want to themselves.

#2. Be honest with yourself

Is this something you can achieve? Sure, your garage band has always dreamed of going on tour, but you have a family to support and a 9-to-5 job that pays the bills. I understand. You may have wanted to play in the NBA, and while you have impressive ball-handling skills or sick handles as the kids say, you're only 5'9" and weigh 140 pounds. While neither of those dreams is impossible, they are unlikely. Not being honest with yourself will only lead to disappointment and frustration for you and those closest to you.

#3. Write it down

According to Jack Flynn and his research on goal setting, only 17% of all people set personal goals. 14% made goals for themselves without writing them down, while the remaining 3% wrote theirs down. **People who set goals are 10x more likely to be successful, and those who write them down are 42% more likely to achieve them.**[1] If you make a goal and write it down, the odds are stacked in your favor, and you put yourself among the elite at setting and keeping goals. Writing it down lights the pathway and paves a runway to achieve goals. Writing it down demonstrates a bit of commitment. Write. It. Down.

Box Jump

The box jump from the Dream Phase to the Plan Phase is **finding the time**. Time is the key. Everyone is busy. The single man with no children is busy. The married mom of 3 is busy, high school students are busy, your retired memaw is busy (though it may not look like it). Everyone is busy. You will always need to find the time to work on your goal. This likely will involve a willingness to sacrifice some of the guilty pleasure time pits. Netflix, Xbox, scrolling social media, or sleeping in may be on the chopping block.

To clear the box, **find a foothold**. A foothold is a rock-climbing term used to describe a strong and firm position. From a foothold one can advance. For us, a foothold is a simple window of time where you can begin planning. If you can establish this foothold then you can begin planning your next move. You can begin answering questions such as:

- When will I work on it?
- How long will I work on it?
- How many days a week?
- What equipment do I need?

These are not questions of grit, perseverance, or desire; they are logistical questions that create a path when answered.

So where can you find this time to create a foothold? Where can you find a consistent 15, 30, 60 minutes each day? Early mornings are the undisputed kings of working on your goal. By using early mornings, your goal has the first fruits of your attention, especially if you have a busy household. Waking up early can give you an hour or two to make progress. In fact, a University of Toronto study finds that morning people are happier and healthier than those who burn the midnight oil.[2] Lunch breaks are another great time to put in 15-30 minutes. Commutes or waiting to pick up your kid in the carline allow margin as well if your goal requires listening to something or having a conversation.[3]

In short, the best way to break free from the Dream Phase is to plan. When you start planning, you begin taking responsibility and greater ownership of your goal.

Here's a challenge for you, especially since it can be hard to find time. My daughter has food allergies, and we were advised to keep a food journal to track what might be causing her issues. I challenge you to journal your time over the course of 3 to 4 days. Don't overthink it; it doesn't need to be fancy—a blank piece of paper will do. Break your day into 30-minute blocks and write down everything you do during those intervals. After 3 to 4 days, you'll identify your 'time thieves'—the activities that rob you of your spare hours. Just as creating a budget helps you manage and track your money; a time journal will help you manage and track your time. Create this foothold for your advance toward the Plan Phase.

3 Questions to Start Poorly

- What is something you would do if you knew you couldn't fail?
- What is a routine you want to make a part of your life?
- I wish I was a person who _____.

The Plan Phase

Y ou break free from the Dream Phase and enter the Plan Phase when you find a foothold and start to answer some questions. This is what you want to do. Here is when you want to begin. These are the materials you'll need.

For example: The person looking to get in shape and change their diet starts making a plan. They circle a day on the calendar. They write down some specific workouts they want to do. They make a meal plan to eat foods that are good for their body. They hire a health coach or find an accountability partner.

They designate the best time of the day for them to work out because they have a busy schedule as is. They also purchase or gather the materials they need to set them up for success, whether that's a fresh pair of running shoes or comfortable athletic gear since they are a few sizes up from the last time they worked out.

Pros of the Plan Phase

The great news is your dreams/habits/goals are becoming realistic. You are measuring what it takes because this goal means THAT much to you. You are naming the specifics of when, where, and how you will do this.

Cons of the Plan Phase

If you are a person who spent a long time in the Dream Phase, you can hide from your goal in the Plan Phase. You can use over-planning as a way of procrastinating and hiding from your goal. There are countless important tasks we want to accomplish each day, yet we often keep ourselves busy with other activities instead of focusing on our goals. Your desire to have every detail in place before you begin can paralyze you from moving forward. Remember, the key is to start, no matter how imperfectly.

Tips to Thrive in the Plan Phase

#1. Create the Menu

Sometimes, we limit ourselves in what we consider progress toward our goals. There are often multiple ways to work on a goal, not just one. Decide what counts. Author Jon Acuff shares an example of his goal to read 100 books in a year. It was his goal, so he got to define what counted. Graphic novels, audiobooks, and more were included. He created a list of what counted, a sort of menu for himself—and you can do the same.

Create a list of different ways you can work on your goal. If you believe that you're only fulfilling your goal by waking up at 5 a.m. to run the same route every day, what happens when it rains, you're traveling, or you don't feel well? You don't have to give up for the day—instead, choose something else from your menu. For example, if your goal is fitness-oriented, stretching can be a valid option on your list. If you're preparing for a presentation but don't have your laptop, use your phone to watch YouTube videos on public speaking tips or learn more about your subject. Just like restaurants offer various options to satisfy your hunger, your goals should have options too.

Harvard scientist Dr Ellen Langer conducted a study where she took 84 hotel maids, took various measurements of these ladies, and split them into two groups. Most of these ladies agreed finding time to exercise after work was difficult due to the physical demands of the job. The first group of 42 was shown how all the things they do at work have a workout/exercise equivalent—walking, folding, scrubbing, etc. They were educated on how their daily routines contributed to their physical fitness.

The second group of 42 were told nothing. After a month, it was found that the ladies in the first group saw a drop in weight, a change in waist-to-hip ratio, a change in BMI, and a lowering in blood pressure. All because they discovered they were exercising more than they thought. They were convinced it counted.[1]

If you think it counts, it counts. Create a menu of what counts.

#2. Name When/Where

As I mentioned, as the first big box jump, finding a foothold of time is the hardest task for most people. "In my free time" never works. Not consistently. If we have dreams or goals, time is never free.

You will always fill your free time with something, and the default is something relaxing or fun. You must establish WHEN you will work on this and how long you will work on it. If you have a goal to dedicate 2 hours a day to something, that's a great goal, but if you currently spend 0 hours on it, then maybe that's a little too ambitious unless you are single and/or have loads of free time. More on this under the Start Phase. Answering the WHERE question allows you to associate that chair, that room, or that table as a place where you get work done. Studies show you shouldn't eat and watch lots of TV in your bed because it affects your ability to use your bed for sleeping. It's the same idea with where you work on your goal. Having a "spot" reminds you why you are in THAT exact place. It's time to get to work.

#3. Make it a game

So many companies have gamified their products, but you don't even realize it. This is not to say that these companies create games, but I can open Papa John's app, and every time I buy a pizza, I get points toward getting a free pizza. This is true for Chick-fil-A, coffee shops, and clothing boutiques. There is a dopamine effect every time you get that small reward. I track habits of my own, and I have a weekly points system that gives me points for doing certain tasks each week. I score them out to a percentage at the end of the week and give myself a grade. This helps me be proactive and intentional. I make it a game. It's fun for me, but it might feel like work and a chore for others. No one else sees it but me, yet it keeps me engaged and shows how I performed that week. It also encourages me to take extra steps on the final day to improve my weekly score. Tie a reward to your goal and set benchmarks along the way to keep it refreshing and engaging.

#4. Carve a path

One of my favorite takeaways from James Clear's *Atomic Habits* is the idea of increasing the friction for habits you want to break and decreasing the friction for those you want to develop. For example, if you want to reduce the time you spend watching Netflix or playing PlayStation, increase the friction. Put your PlayStation in a closet, so you have to take it out and plug it in each time you want to use it. I've even heard of people locking their TV remotes in safes to make watching TV harder. The concept is simple: if it requires more effort, you're less likely to do it. If you really want to play, you'll make the effort to get it out.

Conversely, if you want to go for a walk each morning, decrease the friction. Lay out your shoes and walking clothes the night before to make it as easy as possible the next morning. Set yourself up for success daily. Adjusting the friction can carve a path for your success.

Box Jump

The box jump from the Plan Phase to the Start Phase is **delusion**. More specifically, the delusion of the perfect plan. You think if you have the perfect plan, then you will have the perfect start. Everything will be perfect. The stars will align.

We don't do that here at Start Poorly.

Even if we did and you convince yourself that you have the perfect plan in place, your plan will be destroyed once you actually begin. And sometimes, that can destroy your confidence and morale. In short, there are things outside of your control that will come up. Having a change of mindset will help you drop the delusion of the perfect plan. More on when your plan falls apart later.

To clear the box, **create a simple plan** with a pencil, not a complex plan with a pen. Answering these three questions sets you in the starting position: When, what, and how long.

- When will I start?
- What do I need to start?
- How long will it take for me to work on it when I start?

I believe if you answer those three questions, you will be at that 80% point in your planning. That's enough to start poorly. In this phase, fear tells you that you have to have all the details in place and that your plan needs to be perfect. You think if you don't have everything in place, you'll do it wrong. Over-planning can paralyze you and keep you in the planning phase for too long. Sidestep the perfect plan.

When I began to work on this book, I needed a notebook and a computer. I would work on it for an hour a day. Materials I used along the way changed a little, but not much. Writing every day turned into five days a week, but answering those three questions got me ready for the starting line.

Following the tips above will help you move into the Start Phase. Don't get caught up in the delusion of the perfect plan. There is no perfect plan, and if there was one, it would likely change soon after you start. Drop the delusion and be flexible. Plan simple in pencil, not complex in pen.

3 Questions to Start Poorly

- When is the best time of your day to work on your goal? How much time could you give to it each week?

- What are some specific sacrifices you know you need to make in order to work toward your goal?

- How can you make it a game and reward yourself as you make progress?

8

The Start Phase

T he Start Phase and the Dream Phase can be some of the most exciting times in the process. You have finally begun! There is a thrill and rush as you complete Day 1. You are living out the dream and working towards the goal. You know it will be a long journey, but you feel prepared for it. It's the first day on the job, the first step in a new direction, an introduction to the new you.

Pros of the Start Phase

You are finally beginning your journey, and you have found the courage to move forward no matter how poorly you start, how ugly it looks, or how imperfect the plans are. You are taking ownership. You are taking control. You are doing something about it.

Cons of the Start Phase

The scary part of starting your goal is you are also about to find out if you have what it takes, and that discovery may disappoint you. When you start, you discover what you are made of. Can I do this? What will people say when I tell them what I have started? When you start, people will likely notice. Some may cheer you on and go about their business. Others may think you are naive or be simply indifferent. People's reactions when you tell them may disappoint you. If they seem disinterested, remember you have been spending a long time with this goal, and they are just now hearing about it, and it is very new to them.

Tips to Thrive in the Start Phase

#1. Don't change your life

Put that on a T-shirt, right? That sort of goes against every goal-setting book or mantra you have come across, I'm sure. Starting poorly shouldn't change your life. If you turn your life on its head, that will be incredibly hard to sustain. It's a common mistake people make with diets. They change everything about what they eat and drink rather than make small changes along the way, cutting out one thing at a time to become healthier. The crash diet drops weight but never lasts. If you've always wanted to be an author, you won't likely quit your day job and dedicate all your time to writing. The same goes for starting a small business. Wisdom would tell you to recruit a client here or there and begin with one. If what you want to do will cost you an arm and a leg, maybe there's a cheaper way to do it. Start with the $10 version and not the $60 one— the $100 instead of the $500. Starting poorly should not cost you a lot of money either. There are many with good intentions who have expensive bicycles and hunting gear collecting dust in their garages. There are habits and hobbies we tried to get into that never went anywhere. Your goal should also not take away large chunks of time from your spouse or kids, provided you still want to have them when you are done. When starting something new, it shouldn't dramatically change your life or your wallet—not yet, anyway. Starting poorly means starting simply.

#2. Pivot when it doesn't work

You may find that the plan you developed in the Plan Phase doesn't work or isn't sustainable. This is why we create a plan using a pencil, not a pen. Perhaps you didn't follow the advice from step one. If that's the case, change your routine. Refer back to the menu you created in the Plan Phase. If you see it's not sustainable, adjust your goals to be realistic yet still challenging.

For example, don't abandon your goal of 100 push-ups a day just because you can't keep up or have injured your wrist. Change it to 50 push-ups or switch to a different exercise instead. If you're exercising and find it's becoming overwhelming, a pivot can help you continue without injury. If you're neglecting your family while pursuing new leads for your start-up, pivot when you realize it's too much. Limit yourself to a certain number of calls each day.

If extended family visits for a few days, don't abandon your routine—adapt and pick it up when you can. To maintain your habits and keep your goals moving forward, you must make them sustainable. Be flexible and pivot to sustain your progress.

Box Jump

The box jump from Start to Grind is the easiest box jump to clear because you have to do nothing to find it. It is **resistance**. Like wet cement, resistance slowly hardens into a difficult grind. It's identified when your work is starting to become more difficult. The start-up energy has worn off. The ideas feel dry and stale. It's becoming more difficult to get up early. You begin asking the questions, "Why did I say I would do this?" "Do I really want to do this?"

To clear the box jump, the keyword is **acknowledge**. Simply acknowledge you are entering the Grind Phase. Say it out loud even, "I'm in the Grind Phase now." Acknowledge it's all becoming more difficult. As long as you can recognize the resistance, you can prepare yourself for what is next. A man who knows he's about to walk through a desert can prepare for that desert. You can remind yourself, "This is supposed to be difficult." Though it may feel like a desert, there is life on the other side, and an oasis is along the way. You don't have to do anything to move from the Start Phase to the Grind Phase. The Grind Phase will find you.

3 Questions to Start Poorly

- What are some very little ways you can begin working toward your goal that will not overhaul your life on a massive scale?

- In what ways do you need to pivot with your goal? Did you find some things you need to change to make it more sustainable?

- Do you have a plan that's a little too ambitious at the start? How can you make it more sustainable?

9

The Grind Phase

T he Grind Phase has arrived. It comes after the thrill, fun, and excitement of starting has faded, revealing the true work ahead. This phase separates the amateurs from the professionals and the men from the boys. It tests your commitment, patience, and dedication to the process.

In the Grind Phase, you have been at it for a while, and you have hit roadblocks. Ideas don't seem as fresh, and you hit a creative wall. It's harder to get out of bed so early. You are irritated looking at the same computer screen, same guitar, same pair of running shoes. Coffee isn't energizing you like it once did. This is the stage where it is easiest to give up.

Pros of the Grind Phase

The Grind Phase is rewarding because it develops grit. It makes you dig deep within yourself. It's doing something hard out of commitment and dedication. You aren't fueled by feeling any longer but duty. You know what hard work looks like, your resolve is strengthened, and your Self-Efficacy from Chapter 4 is increasing along the way.

Cons of the Grind Phase

It's hard. Flat out. You want to quit. You might find out you don't have what it takes or at least not willing to commit to what it takes. Fear is back and is now saying, "I told you so."

Fear manifests as doubt and makes you ask yourself a lot of questions:

- Is this going to be any good?
- Will I even finish this?
- Will anyone read this?
- Will anyone hire me?
- Do people even care?

Fear is a post-game reporter asking you all the questions you don't feel like answering after a big loss.

Tips to Thrive in the Grind Phase

#1. Rule of 3

Olympic-level trainers know how to get the best out of their athletes. They also know every athlete feels differently from day to day. According to Olympian Alexi Pappas[1], when she trains, she often feels 1 of 3 ways during a workout.

#1. I feel driven, and I feel like I am truly working toward success.

#2. I'm putting in the work; it's difficult, but it's okay. It's just part of the process.

#3. I hate this; why am I even doing this? I will never win gold.

Pappas learned that most athletes spend 1/3 of their workouts in each of these categories, thus the rule of 3. Understanding the rule of 3 can also help you during the Grind Phase. While working on your goal and while you are in the middle of the difficult grind, make a note of how you think that day went and realize hard, unproductive days are part of the process. This freed me up to have some bad days and not quit. While writing this book, I would rate my feelings about my work on a scale of 1-10. For every 5/10, there was a 7/10. For every 7/10, there was a 9/10. It's okay to give yourself a pass on bad days.

#2. Create the Loop

Create a loop of encouragement and motivation in your life. Find voices with similar interests that motivate you and stir your passions. This will help keep you encouraged and immersed in your work. For example, as a 90s kid, I grew up loving the Teenage Mutant Ninja Turtles. Leonardo was my favorite because he wore blue and was the unofficial leader of the group. Like most boys, I watched the TMNT movies and cartoons, played with the action figures, ate pizza at every turn, and played the video games. What advertisers know is if they can get you in the loop, they have you. When I say "they have you," I mean that they make money off of you (or your parents).

Advertisers know one thing feeds into another. They know how to renew and reengage interest in something if it ever fades with people. When Peter Jackson's *The Lord of the Rings* Trilogy was released, it introduced a new generation to the writings of J.R.R Tolkien and created a new fanbase for Middle Earth enthusiasts. Thousands of new fans began to buy merchandise, play the LOTR games, read *The Hobbit* and even watch the *Rings of*

Power installment on Prime Video. Advertisers create loops for people to constantly be reminded and reengaged with the products they sell.

When it comes to your goal, the more you can make that thing part of your life, the better the chance you have of creating the kind of interest loop you want. Create loops in your life that can constantly stir in you this desire to take the next step and achieve, and it will help you through the Grind Phase. Want to improve your commitment to running? Collect YouTube clips on running tips, find community running groups or Facebook groups dedicated to running. Read, listen, watch, and talk more about running. Discouraged about not losing the weight you want? Listen to some of the stories of people who finally had those big breakthroughs you are looking for. Find people and voices in your niche that can relate to the difficult days of your goal. Those voices can be a refreshing oasis in the desert of the grind.

If I surround myself with people who are encouraging and if I listen to podcasts and channels that speak powerfully about goals I want to develop, it will stir that desire in me greatly. Create that loop within your own life, and you will find voices that speak to you, motivate you, and stir your passions when you get stale and discouraged.

#3. Cut the Wood/Carry the Water

This is a term used by Seth Godin in *The Practice*. In simpler times, a small village always needed water from the well and firewood cut for heating and cooking. You might not need it for that day, but it would be useful eventually.[2] It's not exciting work, but it's work that must be done. This is a message to stick to it. Keep doing it. Keep working. Get up and run the mile even if it won't be your fastest. Sit in front of the keyboard and write for the 30 min you said you would, even if you know it's not headed to any NY Times bestseller list. This is the concept of simply taking action. It may feel like it has little benefit, but it will reap its reward later when you need fresh water and wood to burn. It also builds resolve, which is what you need in this phase.

When to Pause

I want to pause for a moment in the middle of this chapter on the Grind Phase to address something important. Is there ever a good and right time to pause your goal?

Absolutely.

There's wisdom in understanding your current season and accepting your limitations. It does not mean you are a quitter; it does not mean you are a loser. It likely means you are being responsible for yourself and for others.

You might be in a season of life where all of this dream-chasing and goal-setting sounds amazing, but you simply cannot do it right now. That is okay. There might be a time in a different season or in a few years when you can.

This is where you have to draw the line between committed and fanatic. Does your goal isolate you from your family? Does it drive you and your spouse apart? Does it affect your health? Some of the highest achievers in the world have very dysfunctional personal lives because they fail to find a healthy balance in life between achieving success and investing in their families and friends.

If you have a young family and you find that your time is spread very thin, you are not alone. Are you or your spouse pregnant? Get ready to get no sleep, let alone any goals completed. Are you or someone you love sick or injured?

Any of these might be a reason to pause your goal. For obsessive-compulsive or addictive personalities, dreams easily become idols. Keep your priorities straight, especially if you are insecure and trying to prove something.

Tip: If your family feels neglected, try to find ways to incorporate them into your goals, whether it be through conversations about what you are doing or having them join you in your training or lessons. Keeping the lines of communication open with your family and welcoming their feedback on how you're balancing it all is very important. A shared journey is a more memorable one.

Box Jump

The box jump to clear with the Grind Phase is **doubt**. Some of the symptoms of doubt may include fatigue, motivation plateauing, and second-guessing.

"I don't think I can do this."

"I have so much further to go."

"I will never be that good at this."

To clear the box, this is where we use the power of poorly. **Keep moving**. You will have plenty of days when your work feels pointless and fruitless. It doesn't matter. You don't have to be the best, the smartest, or first across the line. All you have to do is remain standing at the end. The goal of CBS's *Survivor* is to be the last person standing. That person is rarely the most charismatic, athletic, or attractive. They won because they stayed on their feet. Video games like *Fortnite* and *Warzone* are designed for you to be the last person alive in the game. Think of *The Hunger Games* to use another pop culture reference. You don't need to have the most kills or be the best player, just the last one standing.

In other words, it doesn't have to be perfect. There will be many days when your efforts and hard work feel meaningless. Keep moving. Hit the spinner, carry the water, remember the rule of 3, and keep yourself in the game.

3 Questions to Start Poorly

- What doubts hit you often on your journey through the Grind Phase?
- What does creating a loop look like for what you want to do?
- What task or actions would you consider, cutting the wood or carrying the water?

10

The Finish Phase

When you emerge from the desert of the grind, you see the end in sight, a light at the end of the tunnel. The Finish Phase can be defined in different ways depending on the goal or dreams you are pursuing. If it's a habit you wish to develop, you are never truly finished, but you are at the finish line of it becoming a consistent habit for you. If it is a specific goal, you are coming close to completing that goal and perfecting your work, and if it's a dream, you are living it. The Start and Grind phases have built, resolved, and refined your process.

It is the final stage of what you sought to do; it is the finishing touch. It's quitting your full-time job to take on your new venture full-time. It's running the marathon you set out to complete. It's entering your canvases into an art show. Sending your final draft to a publisher or playing your music for someone- anyone!

Pros of the Finish Phase

You have come to the end of the goal. You finally are able to check it off your list and experience the satisfaction of a completed job. Your work gets recognition. You can reflect on your journey from start to completion. For Jimmy, reaching the summit of Kilimanjaro was the crowning achievement of his dream, with the half and full marathons as significant benchmarks along the way. Starting poorly paid off.

Cons of the Finish Phase

Finishing may have surprising feelings and consequences. It can be scary. What if people don't like my work? What if I move on, and what comes next? Some, oddly, wish to stay on the edge of completion and never hit the finish button due to fear. Others have found so much of their identity in the journey they fear they will lose that identity once the journey is over. Fear will attack you in each phase, even with a job well done.

Tips to Thrive in the Finish Phase

#1. Sell it

Ship your work. In Godin's *The Practice*, he discusses the importance of shipping what you made for the world.[1] He doesn't mean you make money off your goal or send it somewhere in the mail, though you can; he means believing in what you have done so much that you share it with the world. If it's canvases you paint, put them out to sell. If it's a book to write, don't be ashamed to promote it. If it's playing the guitar, play for someone. If you make a video, you finally upload it. Run a marathon, promote the business, and play with the church band to put your skills out there for others to see. Don't be afraid to complete AND ship your work.

#2. Celebrate It

Make a memory, post a pic, frame the first dollar, and celebrate the moment. Document this moment and write about it in your journal. How might the completion of this goal bridge into your next goal? What doors are now open as a result of this finish?

<u>Box Jump</u>

You wouldn't think there would be much of a box jump to the finish line, but there is a common one. **Perfection.** The idea that you can't finish until it's perfect. Perfectionism still needs to be sidestepped if you are looking to finish. Your work will never be good enough for everyone, but it's already good enough for someone.[2]

For some, the Finish Phase will always be tweaking the business or perfecting the process, but some goals need an official finish line. The marathon runner has a date circled where she will finish her race. The author has the day the book is officially launched. The person who just wants to declutter the garage has a moment when they cross it off their to-do list. Some are also fearful of what finishing might mean. What does the world think of my finished work? Do I have something of value? Did I waste my time? What now?

You can procrastinate through all the phases, including this one. But once again, fear is going to feed you if you eat at its buffet. What's the special offered in the Finish Phase? Rejection pie with a whipped topping of disappointment? Regret Soup? The fear that no one cares, no one will like your product‐ the fear it won't be good enough, that you will have wasted your time?

To clear the box jump, **realize and accept** that it will never be perfect. Set a deadline and hit send anyway. The world is waiting to see the gifts you have to offer.

You and the Phases

The phases are a map to help you plot where you are in your journey. Take a moment and evaluate where you are in any dream or goal you have. The phases should help you establish where you are. And like a map, you can't know where you are going until you know where you are.

3 Questions to Start Poorly

- If working towards a goal, which phase do you find yourself stuck in?
- What box do you need to jump to move on?
- What is difficult for you to finalize and move on from?

11

What's Left?

T he only thing left to do is to start poorly. This book is an invitation to start. But not just to start. It's permission to be terrible when you start. It's an invitation to start no matter how badly or imperfectly or how small that start may be. You may feel like your start is more of a stumble, but by starting poorly, you are stumbling in the right direction. Life is too short. Go and risk being bad at something and follow your dream.

After all, when was the last time you did something for the first time? I bet you were a better parent to your third kid than you were with your first. I bet you brush your teeth better today than you did when you were 5. I'd wager you can tie your shoes tighter and faster than you could when you were 8. There are so many other places in life where you have no option other than to start poorly. You had to start from nothing because we all have to start somewhere.

What year is it?

In 1981, Harvard scientist Dr. Ellen Langer[1] from chapter 7 did a study where she took two groups of men in their 70s and 80s to a remote monastery.

She took the first group away for a week and asked them to talk about life 22 years prior. She wanted them to remember what the world was like, the memories they had of that time, what was popular, etc. To essentially live in the present day but reminisce.

She asked the second group of men to not just talk about life 22 years prior but also pretend they were 22 years younger for a week. Live in 1959. She wanted them to think, act, and behave as if they still lived in 1959.

She hung up old pictures of markers in their lives in the late 1950s. There were pictures of the Kennedy brothers, Nat King Cole, and Marilyn Monroe. Copies of *Life* and the *Saturday Evening Post* were scattered about. These men had discussions about sports legends like Mickey Mantle and Floyd Patterson, they talked of Castro's victory ride through Havana, and Nikita Khrushchev and the need for bomb shelters.

Before and after the experiment, these men took a series of cognitive and physical tests, and after just one week, there were dramatic positive changes across the board. These men were stronger and more flexible. Height, weight, posture, hearing, vision— even their performance on intelligence tests had improved. Their joints were more flexible, their shoulders wider, their fingers not only more agile but longer and less gnarled by arthritis.

But the men who had acted as if they were actually back in 1959 showed significantly more improvement than those who had just reminisced about it. Those who had impersonated younger men seemed to have bodies that actually *were* younger.

The ability of the mind is powerful, but there is a difference between pretending to be someone and actually becoming that person. You have the opportunity not just to pretend but to become the person you want to be. To fulfill the dream inside you and complete the goal before you.

Become that person.

Start today... Poorly, if need be.

Epilogue

T owards the completion of this book, my wife asked me, "What was your goal in writing this book?

"What do you mean?" I asked.

"Well, was it to become a published author? To make money? Was it to help people? Or was it to simply accomplish the goal of writing a book?"

I stopped and thought for a moment because I had forgotten. I had taken so many steps forward in its development and learned about formatting, publishing, cover design, marketing, and pricing. I had to think long and hard.

And that's when it hit me.

I just wanted to develop my writing skills by making writing a daily habit. If what I wrote helped people, then I wanted to do my part.

That's how it started; I began dedicating myself to writing for an hour a day. When Saturdays and Sundays got hard, I pivoted and only wrote five days a week. I didn't give up. Even though 5 hours a week isn't as good as 7, it's still better than 0.

While writing this book, I experienced each phase along the way. I **dreamed** of developing a writing habit that could one day become a book. I developed a simple **plan** to get started. When I got **started**, I was flexible and changed what worked for me. I had many days where writing felt like a **grind**· more of a chore than a joy. However, the rule of 3 still remained true. For all the 5/10 days I had, there were just as many 7/10 days and 9/10 days. I hit the spinner each day, and if I only got one, I still moved forward. And lastly, as I got closer and closer to the finish line, I felt the fear of shipping my work. I felt nervous as friends read through my beta scripts and gave feedback.

What started with a habit turned into a completed goal, and we'll see what comes next.

What is your Start Poorly?

As I've highlighted, we have all started poorly somewhere along the way. I would love nothing more than to hear your own Start Poorly story. Head over to justingrifford.com and share your story with me. You can find me on Facebook and follow me on Instagram as well.

About of Author

Justin Grifford is a goal enthusiast and has been shaped in many ways by personal goals he has begun poorly. He and his wife Stacie live in Columbus, MS with their 3 kids where he pastors a church.

Acknowledgements

Special thanks to...

Ashley Leonard, Rick Dinkins, Mark Smith, Willie McDonald, Josh Austin, Clint O'Neal, and Jonathan Hart, thank you for your valuable feedback in making this book the best it can be. Special thanks to Jimmy Shaw for taking the time to share his story. Again, go check out discipletrek.org and book a trip with him.

To my parents, Tim & Mary Grifford, thank you for all your love and support over the years to do the things I have felt called to do. And to my wife Stacie whose love and life-giving words made me push forward. And to my sweet children, I cherish each of you.

Notes

Introduction

1. This is a quote by Eric Koester from Manuscripts.com that I believe to be so true. We like things that are familiar but with a different take.

Chapter 1: Always Late

1. Jon Acuff, *All it Takes is a Goal.* (Grand Rapids: Baker Books. 2023) 16

Chapter 3: Start Poorly

1. Jon Acuff, Finish: Give Yourself the Gift of Done (Hampstead: Portfolio 2017)
2. Denzel Washington, "Fail Big" Dillard University 2015 Commencement Address https://www.youtube.com/watch?v=ROiNPUwg9Q.
3. Denzel Washington, University of Pennsylvania 2011 Commencement Address https://www.youtube.com/watch?v=vpW2sGlCtaE
4. Gillian Zoe Segal, *Getting There: A Book of Mentors* (ABRAMS Image; Illustrated edition, 2015).
5. Jeff and Jami Downs, *Streaking: The Simple Practice of Conscious, Consistent Actions That*

Create Life-Changing Results. (Canada, Page Two, 2020.)

Chapter 4:   The Science of Confidence

1. Rosenshine, B., & Stevens, R. (1984). Classroom instruction in reading. In P. D. Pearson (Ed.), Recent research on reading. New York: Longman.

Chapter 5:   Couch to Kilimanjaro

1. J.K. Rowling, 'The Fringe Benefits of Failure, and the Importance of Imagination' June 6th, 2008. https://news.harvard.edu/gazette/story/2008/06/te xt-of-j-k-rowling-speech/

Chapter 6:   The Dream Phase

1. Jack Flynn, "15+ Essential Goal-Setting Statistics [2023]: The Importance of Setting Goals," December 11th, 2023. https://www.zippia.com/advice/goal-setting-statistics/#:~:text=We%E2%80%99ve%20gathere d%20all%20the%20latest%20goal-setting%20statistics%2C%20and,peers%20increa se%20their%20chance%20of%20success%20by%2 040%25.
2. Jessica McDiarmid, "University of Toronto Sleep Study Says Early Birds are Happier, Healthier," *Toronto Star,* June 27th, 2012,

http://www.thestar.com/news.gta/2012/06/27/
university_of_toronto_sleep_study_says_early_
birds_are_happier_healthier.html.
3. Jessica Turner, The Fringe Hours (Grand
Rapids: Baker Publishing, 2015),119.

Chapter 7:   The Plan Phase

1. Alix Spiegel "Hotel Maids Challenge the Placebo
Effect" NPR January 3rd, 2008,
https://www.npr.org/2008/01/03/17792517/hotel-
maids-challenge-the-placebo-effect

Chapter 9:   The Grind Phase

1. Jessica Stillman, "Use This Olympians Rule of
Thirds to Chase Any Big Dream," Inc. June 6th,
2022, https://www.inc.com/jessica-stillman/alexi-
pappas-goal-setting-rule-of-thirds.html.
2. Seth Godin, The Practice: Shipping Creative
Work (Penguin Audio) 2020.

Chapter 10:   The Finish Phase

1. Godin, The Practice: Shipping Creative Work
2. Godin, The Practice: Shipping Creative Work

Chapter 11:   What's Left?

1. Cara Feinberg, "The Mindfulness Chronicles:
The Psychology of Possibility" Harvard

Magazine, Sept/Oct 2010,
https://www.harvardmagazine.com/2010/08/the-mindfulness-chronicles